21st
Century
Skills Library

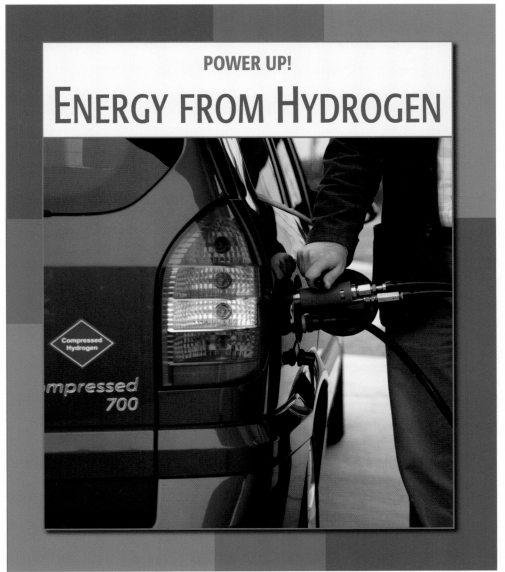

POWER UP!

ENERGY FROM HYDROGEN

Compressed
Hydrogen

mpressed
700

David Lippman

DESERONTO
PUBLIC LIBRARY

Cherry Lake Publishing
Ann Arbor, Michigan

CHERRY LAKE
Publishing

Published in the United States of America by Cherry Lake Publishing
Ann Arbor, MI
www.cherrylakepublishing.com

Photo Credits: Cover, © Brooks Kraft/Corbis; Title Page, © Brooks Kraft/Corbis;
Page 28, © Arctic-Images/CORBIS

Library of Congress Cataloging-in-Publication Data
Lippman, David.
  Energy from hydrogen / by David Lippman.
      p. cm.—(Power up!)
  Includes index.
    ISBN-13: 978-1-60279-048-3 (lib. bdg.)   978-1-60279-095-7 (pbk.)
    ISBN-10: 1-60279-048-5 (lib. bdg.)   1-60279-095-7 (pbk.)
  1. Hydrogen as fuel—Juvenile literature. I. Title. II. Series.
  TP359.H8L56 2008
  665.8'1—dc22   2007007722

*Cherry Lake Publishing would like to acknowledge the work of
The Partnership for 21st Century Skills.
Please visit www.21stcenturyskills.org for more information.*

TABLE OF CONTENTS

CHAPTER ONE

The Problems with Fossil Fuels   4

CHAPTER TWO

The Science of Energy Hydrogen   11

CHAPTER THREE

Manufacturing Hydrogen   16

CHAPTER FOUR

Using Energy Hydrogen   23

Glossary   30

For More Information   31

Index   32

THE PROBLEMS WITH FOSSIL FUELS

Cars that run on fossil fuels make our air dirty. The carbon is also thought to cause global warming.

Joji stepped slowly onto the school bus. He stared straight ahead,

unsmiling. He threw his backpack down in front of him and slumped

down on the seat next to Miriam. He didn't say a word.

"Hey," said Miriam. "You don't look very happy. What's going on?"

When Joji didn't answer, Miriam became concerned. During the entire

trip to school, Joji sat without speaking.

When the bus let them off in front of the school, Miriam tried again to talk with Joji. "What's the matter? Can I help?"

Joji looked at Miriam as if it were the first he had noticed her. "Sorry," he said. "It was yesterday's classes. First, it was Mrs. Garcia's science class and then my social studies class with Mr. Hardin. And my current-events lesson wasn't any better."

Miriam was confused. She said, "You're one of the best students in the whole school. I can't believe you're having trouble with your classes."

Joji smiled for the first time. "That's not it," he said. "It's what we talked about in class. It just hit me

that there are a lot of problems in the world that nobody seems to be able to solve. It kind of freaked me out. What's it going to be like when we grow up? Our lives might be really different than they are today."

The two of them walked slowly toward the front door of the school.

Miriam asked, "What did you guys talk about?"

Millions of Americans travel to and from their jobs by car every week—and create air pollution in the process.

"In science class, Mrs. Garcia said that the world was starting to run out of oil and coal. She said that scientists aren't quite sure when supplies will start getting smaller, but it will happen. She said that we needed to practice **conservation**. We need to take better care of the gasoline we have and use less of it."

"Then Mrs. Garcia said that it might be a good thing that we're going to run out of gas. That's because using gasoline causes pollution. And she said that burning coal to make electricity isn't any better."

"In social studies, it was strange. Mr. Hardin started talking about pollution, too. We were studying **climate**. He said that **carbon** gases from

Miriam was surprised that Joji studied about climate change and the environment in both social studies and science class. Why might you learn about the environment in two different classes?

burning oil and coal were changing the world's climate by making it warmer. Nobody is really sure how fast the world might warm, but most scientists think we need to start putting less carbon in the air. That means burning less gasoline and coal."

"That *is* weird," said Miriam. "I never thought that something you'd learn in science class would have anything to do with social studies class."

"It gets even stranger," said Joji. "When we talked about current events, Brendan brought in a story that he saw in a magazine. It said that our country was being hurt because we were buying so much oil from other countries. The article said that the

Many scientists say that the melting of arctic ice and resulting icebergs are clear examples of global warming.

president wanted people to end their **addiction** to foreign oil. Brendan said that people are addicted when they keep on using something that they know is harmful."

"Wait!" said Miriam. "I have an idea. You should ask Mrs. Garcia and Mr. Hardin if there's a way to change things."

"You're right," said Joji. "Maybe they have an answer."

Tankers such as this one deliver much of the United States'
oil from countries around the world.

CHAPTER TWO

THE SCIENCE OF ENERGY HYDROGEN

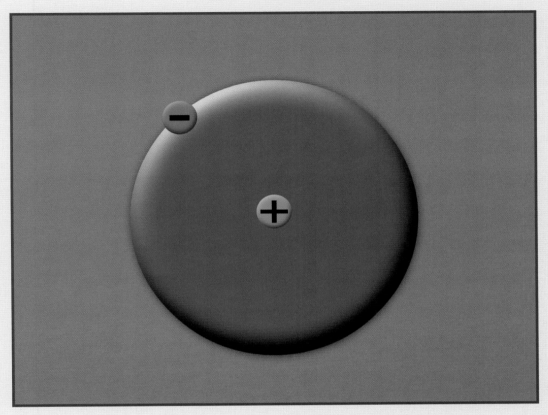

*The Sun's energy comes from hydrogen. Without it, the Sun could
not generate the energy necessary for life on Earth.*

As soon as everyone sat down in science class, Joji raised his hand. When

Mrs. Garcia called on him, he said, "Is there a form of energy that doesn't

pollute? And is there one that we'll never use up?"

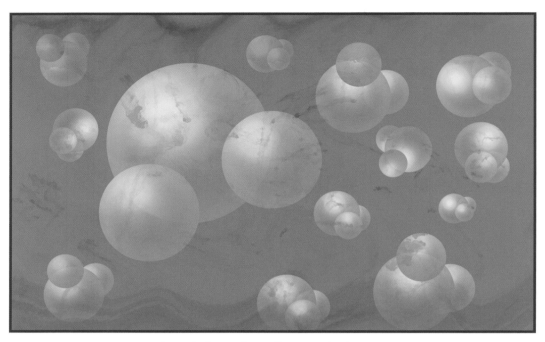

The only byproduct of burning hydrogen is water—H$_2$O—shown here in an artist's drawing.

Mrs. Garcia smiled and said, "There might be. Can you believe that there's a fuel that produces three times as much energy as gasoline? When this fuel is burned, the only product is water. This fuel is called *energy hydrogen,* and that's what we're going to learn about today."

Mrs. Garcia explained how **hydrogen** could be used to deliver energy to vehicles and factories.

"Hydrogen is the smallest and lightest element in the universe. It also is the universe's most common element. About 90 percent of the world's **atoms** are hydrogen. The hydrogen atom is made up of one **proton** and one **electron**. The second smallest element, helium, is four times heavier than hydrogen.

"Hydrogen is a gas at normal temperatures on Earth. However, very little hydrogen gas can be found in Earth's atmosphere. Hydrogen is so light that free hydrogen quickly flies away from Earth into space. Also, hydrogen atoms combine easily with other elements. As a result, only about one in two million atoms in Earth's atmosphere is hydrogen."

21st Century Content

As new energy sources are developed, people will use less oil in the 21st century. However, many more people will earn their livings in the energy business. When people find new ways to create, store, and deliver energy, new jobs will be created.

Hydrogen is a common element. It is found in every breath we take and every glass of water we drink.

"There's more hydrogen on Earth's surface. It is part of all living things.

It also can be found in many chemical compounds. But the most common

source of hydrogen on Earth is water. Water is made up of two atoms of

hydrogen and one atom of **oxygen:** H_2O."

"Because hydrogen does not occur in its free form on Earth, it must be manufactured from other materials. Therefore, scientists say that hydrogen is not an energy source. They describe hydrogen as an energy carrier. It stores and carries energy in a form that can easily be used later on.

"When hydrogen combines with oxygen and a spark, the two gases create a great deal of energy. The reaction also forms water. That's the beauty of hydrogen as energy. There is no pollution and no carbon gases that add to **global warming**."

Hydrogen makes up most of the material of the Sun. The hydrogen gas fuels the nuclear reactions that make the Sun so hot. On Earth, scientists are unlocking secrets about hydrogen as a fuel. How do you think studying the Sun has helped?

CHAPTER THREE

MANUFACTURING HYDROGEN

*Fertilizer plants in the United States make large quantities of hydrogen.
It is currently used in fertilizers but not widely in fuel.*

Atasha's hand shot up in the air. "You said that hydrogen must be created from other materials because it doesn't exist in its free form on Earth. How is hydrogen produced?"

Mrs. Garcia said, "There are several ways that hydrogen can be made.

"The first thing to keep in mind is that hydrogen is most easily made from organic molecules or from water. The organic molecules that can be used include natural gas, coal, and biomass.

"To understand hydrogen production, you also need to know about a law of nature called *the conservation of energy*. This law states that energy

Hybrid cars use less gasoline because batteries provide some of the power. The engines use gasoline more efficiently as well. How would you react if the government required everyone to buy hybrid cars or ones fueled by hydrogen?

cannot be created or destroyed. This means that we need as much energy to produce hydrogen as we can get from using it. Actually, it takes a lot more energy to create hydrogen because some energy is lost in the process.

Scientists are trying to find ways to use less energy and to reduce the cost of creating hydrogen.

The United States has huge resources of coal, which the gasification process could turn into energy that does not add to global warming.

"Almost all of the hydrogen produced today uses natural gas and super-heated steam. This is a process with many steps called *natural gas reforming*.

"A similar process called **gasification** uses coal or biomass to produce hydrogen. Scientists are studying ways to capture the carbon gases during this process. That means that no harmful gases enter the atmosphere. We could use coal to create energy with no effect on global warming.

"Another way to make hydrogen gas is to use an electric current to separate the hydrogen from water. This is a simple process called **electrolysis**. It takes a lot of energy to make hydrogen gas in this way. However, we could use renewable energy sources to produce the electricity. That would allow us to use extra wind or solar energy to create hydrogen that could be stored."

Learning & Innovation Skills

The water from nuclear power plants can be used to make hydrogen for energy. Do you think that this is a good reason to build new nuclear power plants in the United States?

"Nuclear reactors can also be used to make hydrogen. These reactors create a great deal of heat, which is cooled with water. This causes the water to get very hot. The super-heated water then can be split into hydrogen and oxygen with much less energy."

Mrs. Garcia looked up at the clock. "We have a few minutes. Do any of you have questions?"

Joji was the first to raise his hand. "Is hydrogen safe? I remember a TV show about a blimp or something that blew up. The announcer said it blew up because they used hydrogen."

"You saw a show about the airship *Hindenburg*. Hydrogen is far too dangerous to be used in a

20

Some 36 of the 97 people on board the Hindenburg
died in the disaster on May 6, 1937.

balloon or blimp," said Mrs. Garcia. "A leak and a spark might cause a fire.

However, hydrogen gas tanks in cars are quite safe. In fact, hydrogen is

safer than gasoline in an accident. The light hydrogen gas would escape

harmlessly into the air."

"I have one more question," Joji said, just as the bell rang. "When do you think we'll be able to produce hydrogen?"

"You'd be surprised how much hydrogen is produced already," said Mrs. Garcia. "The United States makes enough hydrogen today to fuel 34 million cars. However, the hydrogen isn't used for fuel. It's used to make fertilizer."

CHAPTER FOUR

USING HYDROGEN ENERGY

*For hydrogen-powered cars to become practical in the
United States, there would have to be a nationwide
system of places for drivers to buy the fuel.*

Joji couldn't wait to get to Mr. Hardin's social studies class. When he

came in the door, he went up to Mr. Hardin's desk. "You don't have to

Hydrogen is always stored in sturdy metal tanks.

worry about global warming any more," Joji said with a smile. "Energy

hydrogen is going to replace gasoline. Cars won't make greenhouse gases.

They'll release water instead!"

"Wait a second," said Mr. Hardin. "Let's talk about this when all the class gets seated."

Joji went to his seat and waited to hear what Mr. Hardin had to say. He couldn't believe that Mr. Hardin had doubts about hydrogen.

"Yesterday, we talked about global warming and climate change," Mr. Hardin began. "Today, we're going to talk about energy hydrogen for cars. Will we be able to replace gasoline with hydrogen? Hydrogen energy could work, but it has problems.

"Hydrogen is hard to store. As a gas, it takes up a lot of room. Hydrogen can be cooled to make it liquid. The liquid would take up less space. However,

21st Century Content

Estimates indicate that hydrogen for cars would have to cost about the same as gasoline. The cheapest hydrogen today is made from wind power. It costs about $3.70 per gallon. However, the costs might change significantly as ways of creating usable hydrogen are improved.

you must cool hydrogen to −253°C before it becomes a liquid. In either case, you'd be adding a lot of weight to a car. That would make it expensive to use. Besides, hydrogen gas is very light and would leak out of almost any storage tank."

"One idea is to use metals that capture hydrogen for storage. But the weight of the metal would add weight to the car. That probably won't work either.

"The best idea for cars is the hydrogen fuel cell. A fuel cell is a special kind of battery. It separates the electron from the hydrogen atom's proton. The flow of electrons produces electricity that can power a car motor."

*Hydrogen-powered cars might store the fuel in
the trunk or inside the car seats.*

"Hydrogen fuel cells create no gases. Fuel cells would be used with a

gasoline-powered engine similar to a current hybrid car. However, cars

with fuel cells would be 50 percent more efficient than current hybrid cars.

They would be twice as efficient as a gasoline-powered car."

Cities such as Amsterdam, Barcelona, London, Mexico City, Cairo, and Reykjavik are now experimenting with fuel cell buses.

"Fuel cells sound great, but they cost a lot to make. Right now, they often break and don't last very long. We still have a long way to go before we all can start using hydrogen to power our cars."

"Hydrogen-powered cars are real, however. Some carmakers haves built cars that run on liquid hydrogen. One of these cars is as fast as a race car."

The bell rang, and Joji walked to the school bus. When he saw Miriam, she asked, "How did your classes go?"

"Not bad," said Joji. "We didn't solve global warming. We didn't find a way to keep us from running out of oil. We didn't find a way to stop buying foreign oil. But we learned that there is hope. I know that our future will be different. But maybe it won't be so bad."

One of the important skills you develop as you grow up is how to make good decisions. Here are some you might have to make: Will I drive a smaller car? Will I use public transportation instead of driving?

GLOSSARY

addiction (uh-DIK-shuhn) use of a habit-forming substance, even though the user knows it to be harmful

atoms (AT-uhms) very tiny material units that can be the source of nuclear energy

carbon (KAHR-buhn) element that is part of coal, petroleum, limestone, carbonates, and organic compounds

climate (KLAHY-mit) average condition of the weather at a place over a period of years

conservation (kon-ser-VEY-shuhn) careful saving and protecting of something, especially a natural resource

electrolysis (i-lek-TROL-uh-sis) production of chemical changes by passage of an electric current through a substance

electron (i-LEK-tron) negatively charged part of an atom

gasification (gas-uh-fuh-KEY-shuhn) conversion of a substance into gas

global warming (GLOH-buhl WAWRM-eng) increase in the temperature of Earth's atmosphere and oceans caused by an increase of greenhouse gases in the air

hydrogen (HAHY-druh-juhn) simplest and lightest of all elements

oxygen (OK-si-juhn) reactive element found in water, most rocks, and as a gas in the atmosphere

proton (PROH-ton) positively charged part of an atom

For More Information

Books

Hoffman, Peter. *Tomorrow's Energy: Hydrogen, Fuel Cells, and the Prospects for a Cleaner Planet.* Cambridge, MA: The MIT Press, 2002.

Ewing, Rex A. *Hydrogen: Hot Stuff Cool Science--Journey to a World of Hydrogen Energy and Fuel Cells at the Wasserstoff Farm.* Masonville, CO: Pixyjack Press, 2004.

Walker, Niki. *Hydrogen: Running on Water (Energy Revolution).* New York: Crabtree Publishing Company, 2007.

Hayhurst, Chris. *Hydrogen Power of the Future: New Ways of Turning Fuel Cells into Energy (The Library of Future Energy).* New York: Rosen Publishing Group, 2003.

Haugen, David M. *Hydrogen (Fueling the Future).* San Diego: Greenhaven Press, 2006.

Other Media

Hydrogen Hawaii. DVD. Virtual Image Media Services, 2006.

For an easy-to-understand guide to energy hydrogen, go to the Energy Kids Page of the Department of Energy at *http://www.eia.doe.gov/kids/energyfacts/ sources/IntermediateHydrogen.html*

Learn about the hydrogen energy program of the Department of Energy at *http://www.hydrogen.energy.gov/*

See facts and pictures about a real hydrogen car at *http://www.bmwworld.com/hydrogen/*

INDEX

addiction, 10
air pollution, 6, 8
atoms, 13

biomass, 17, 18
Bulgaria, 19

Canada, 19
carbon gases, 7–8, 19
cars, hydrogen-powered, 23, 26–29
climate, 7
coal, 17, 18
conservation, 7, 17–18

electricity, 6, 17, 19, 24
electrolysis, 19–20
electrons, 13
energy hydrogen, 12, 15

fertilizer plants, 16
fossil fuels, 4, 7
fuel cells, 26–29

gas, 17, 18
gasification, 18
global warming, 5, 15, 19, 24, 25, 29
greenhouse gases, 5, 24

H_2O, 14
helium, 13
Hindenburg, 20–22
hybrid cars, 17, 27

hydrogen
  availability of, 14
  cars powered by, 23, 26–29
  costs, 25
  danger of, 20–21
  energy hydrogen, 12, 15
  fuel cells, 26–29
  manufacture of, 15, 16–22
  storage of, 25–26
  uses for, 12–13

Japan, 19

Kyoto Protocol, 5, 19

Lithuania, 19

natural gas reforming, 18
nuclear power, 20

oil, 7–10, 13, 29
oxygen, 14

pollution, 6, 8,15
protons, 13

Slovakia, 19
solar energy, 19
steam, 18
sun, 11, 15

United States, 19, 20

water, 12, 14, 17, 20
wind energy, 19, 20

ABOUT THE AUTHOR

David Lippman has written and edited books on science, history, and government for more than 20 years. He makes his home in the middle of oil country, Austin, Texas, but looks forward to a time when people will be using clean energy sources.

21st Century Skills Library

Today we depend on gasoline and other petroleum products for much of our energy. However, those energy sources might not last forever. Look inside to explore how scientists are tapping an alternative energy source – corn and other grains – to make ethanol to fuel cars.

The *Power Up!* series introduces readers to important concepts and information needed to understand the quest energy and alternative energy sources in the 21st century. Other titles in the series include:

- Bio-fuels
- Electric Power Grid
- Energy from Wind, Sun, and Tides
- Geothermal Energy
- Hydroelectric Energy
- Nuclear Energy
- Searching for Oil

To guide your reading, look for these notes that will help build the understanding and skills you'll need in the 21st Century. Look for the following margin notes:

 Learning and Innovation skills

You need to learn about lots of things, but you also need to learn how to learn. These notes give you hints about how to use what you know in better and more creative ways.

 21st Century Content

You study reading, math, science, and social studies. You also need to learn about the world of work and your community. These notes tell you about business and money. They also give you ideas about how you can help yourself, your community, and the world.

 Life and Career skills

These notes tell you about skills you will use throughout your life. They give you ideas about how to work well with others, make good decisions, and achieve your goals in life.

CHERRY LAKE Publishing

ISBN-13: 978-1-60279-095-7
ISBN-10: 1-60279-095-7

9 781602 790957

T2-AFZ-084